Education *in* California

Gretchen L. H. O'Brien, M.Ed.

Consultants

Kristina Jovin, M.A.T.
Alvord Unified School District
Teacher of the Year

Vanessa Gunther, Ph. D.
Department of History
Chapman University

Publishing Credits

Rachelle Cracchiolo, M.S.Ed., *Publisher*
Conni Medina, M.A.Ed., *Managing Editor*
Emily R. Smith, M.A.Ed., *Series Developer*
June Kikuchi, *Content Director*
Marc Pioch, M.A.Ed., and Susan Daddis, M.A.Ed., *Editors*
Courtney Roberson, *Senior Graphic Designer*

Image Credits: p.4 California Digital Newspaper Collection; p.5 (top) Courtesy of the Braun Research Library Collection, Autry Museum, Los Angeles; P.32405, (full page) The British Library; pp.6–7 Library of Congress [LC-DIG-pga-00311]; p.7 (top) San Francisco History Center, San Francisco Public Library; p.8 (bottom) Tom Munnecke/Getty Images; pp.8–9, 29 (top) Creative Commons Attribution-Share Alike 3.0 Unported by Falcorian; p.10 Justin Sullivan/Getty Images; p.12 ZUMA Press, Inc./Alamy Stock Photo; p.13 Tower Glass Inc. p.14 Chloe Aftel/Contour by Getty Images; p.16 Jonathan Nackstrand/AFP/Getty Images; pp.18–19 USC Libraries. California Historical Society Collection, 1860-1960; pp.20 (bottom), 21 (top), 29 (middle) Stanford University Libraries, Historical Photograph Collection; p.22 Archive Photos/Getty Images; p.23 NCAA Photos/Getty Images; p.25 NASA; p.26 Jamie Schwaberow/NCAA Photos via Getty Images; pp.26–27, 32 Wally Skalij/Los Angeles Times via Getty Images; pp.28–29 Tara Ziemba/Getty Images; p.29 (bottom) Jamie Schwaberow/NCAA Photos via Getty Images; all other images from iStock and/or Shutterstock.

Teacher Created Materials

5301 Oceanus Drive
Huntington Beach, CA 92649-1030
http://www.tcmpub.com

ISBN 978-1-4258-3246-9
© 2018 Teacher Created Materials, Inc.
Printed in China
Nordica.012019.CA21801586

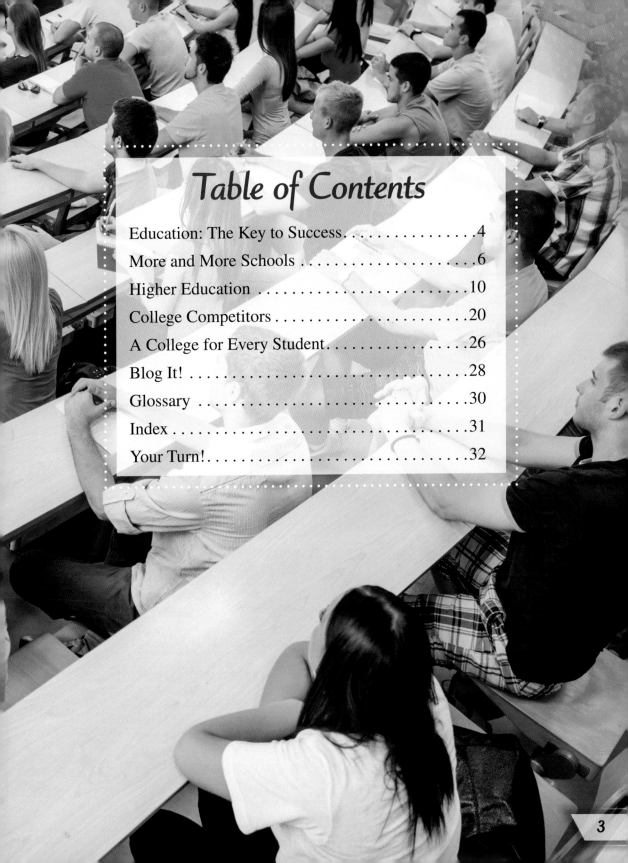

Table of Contents

Education: The Key to Success

California is home to the largest school system in the country. A school system includes all grades from kindergarten through college. Millions of students are in schools every day.

The state's schools had a simple start. Early settlers felt school was **crucial** for a strong community. Olive Isbell was one of those people. She opened the first U.S. school in Santa Clara in 1846. This was before California was even a state. Three years later, a **delegate** named Robert Semple gave a speech. He spoke about the importance of schools. He said that good schools would be the key to the state's success. Many people agreed with him. His speech paved the way for the school system the state has today.

Five years after Isbell's school, the state's first colleges opened their doors. Now, the state is home to some of the best colleges in the world.

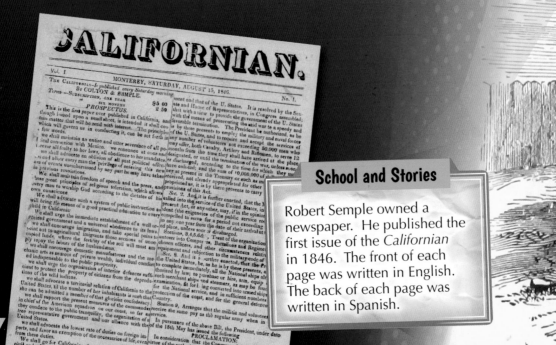

School and Stories

Robert Semple owned a newspaper. He published the first issue of the *Californian* in 1846. The front of each page was written in English. The back of each page was written in Spanish.

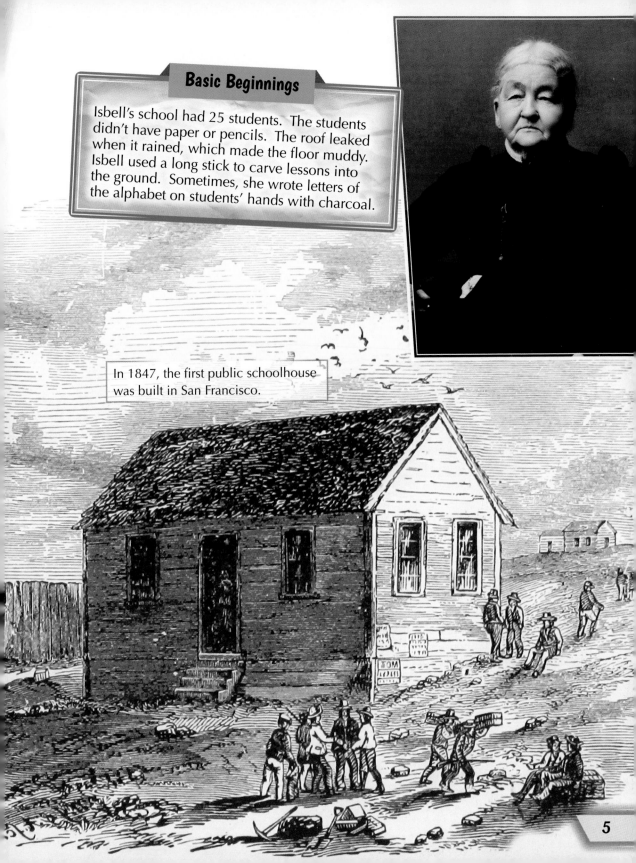

Basic Beginnings

Isbell's school had 25 students. The students didn't have paper or pencils. The roof leaked when it rained, which made the floor muddy. Isbell used a long stick to carve lessons into the ground. Sometimes, she wrote letters of the alphabet on students' hands with charcoal.

In 1847, the first public schoolhouse was built in San Francisco.

More and More Schools

The 1800s were a time of growth for California. Many people moved west hoping to strike it rich. Those settlers wanted a better future for their families. They saw schools as a way to get the lives they wanted. Settlers also pushed for schools to be free. People paid taxes to keep schools free. Today, public schools are still free.

From the 1850s to the 1870s, school lasted three months each year. Students received a very basic education. They attended elementary school. If they wanted to go past that, their families had to pay for it. In the early 1850s, the number of people in the state was growing. There was a need for more schools and teachers. The first "normal" school was founded in 1857. Normal schools were schools that taught people how to be teachers. These schools **evolved** into the college system.

Mendez v. Westminster

In the 1940s, Sylvia Mendez wanted to go to school. When she tried to attend a school in Orange County, she was not allowed. The school was for white students only. The Mendez family, along with four other families, fought for change. They went to court and won. In 1947, the U.S. Court of Appeals ruled to end **segregation** of Mexican students in California's schools. It was the first state to do so.

Civics

Dual Language

Dual-language schools teach students in English and a second language at the same time. There are more than 50,000 students enrolled in these schools in California. Spanish, Mandarin, and Korean are the top three languages taught. The goal is to be able to know and use both languages by the end of fifth grade.

The first normal school later became San Jose State University.

More people came to the state. The school system had to grow as well. Settlers built more elementary schools to keep up. Families paid for their children to go to high school. Soon, more high schools were built. Students wanted to keep going to school beyond high school. Colleges filled that need.

Minn's Evening Normal School opened in the mid-1800s. When it was first built, it was a private normal school for teachers. In 1862, it became a state public school. A new building was needed at this time. San Jose was selected for its new site. It was renamed San Jose State University. This was the first campus of what would become the new California State University (CSU) system.

In 1868, the first University of California (UC) campus opened in Oakland. Classes began the next year. When it opened, the school had only 40 students. It later became UC Berkeley. Today, it is ranked as one of the best universities in the country.

Berkeley's Very Own

Steve Wozniak was a student at UC Berkeley. Through a friend, he met a man named Steve Jobs. The two Steves shared a love of technology and became good friends. In 1976, they started a computer company. After going back and forth for a while, they picked a name for their business—Apple®.

Economics

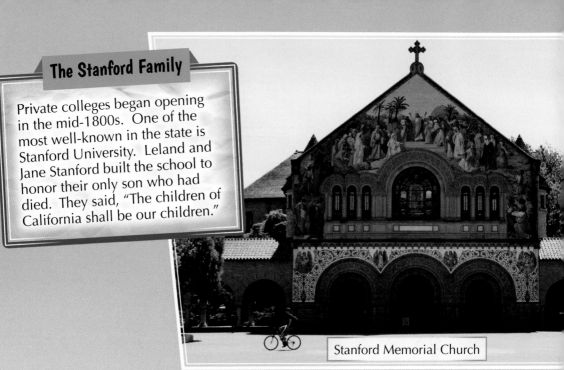

The Stanford Family

Private colleges began opening in the mid-1800s. One of the most well-known in the state is Stanford University. Leland and Jane Stanford built the school to honor their only son who had died. They said, "The children of California shall be our children."

Stanford Memorial Church

South Hall was built in 1873 and is the oldest building on the UC Berkeley campus.

Higher Education

The state's higher education system grew out of need. Any schooling after high school is called *higher education*. Students are not required to go to college. But if someone chooses to go in California, he or she has many choices.

California has hundreds of college campuses. With so many choices, it is important to know about each one. There are three main types of colleges in California.

The first is community college. Students usually go to these schools for two years. The second type is the state college system. It is made up of the CSU and UC campuses. The third is private college. Students typically go to state and private schools for four years.

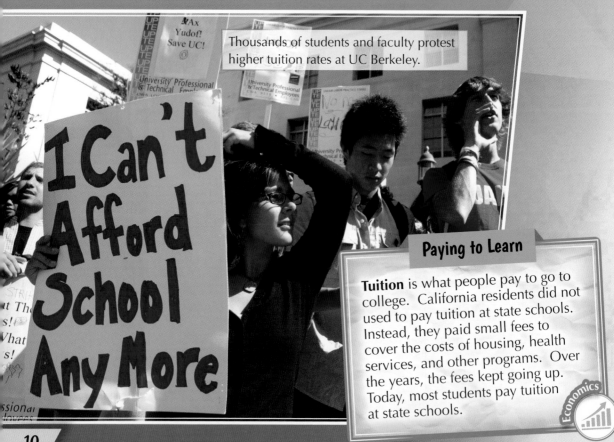

Thousands of students and faculty protest higher tuition rates at UC Berkeley.

Paying to Learn

Tuition is what people pay to go to college. California residents did not used to pay tuition at state schools. Instead, they paid small fees to cover the costs of housing, health services, and other programs. Over the years, the fees kept going up. Today, most students pay tuition at state schools.

What's the Difference?

After high school, students can continue going to school. Colleges are where students can earn their associate's or bachelor's **degrees**. Students at universities can earn those degrees, too. Plus, they can earn their master's degrees or doctorates. People tend to use the word *college* for all these schools.

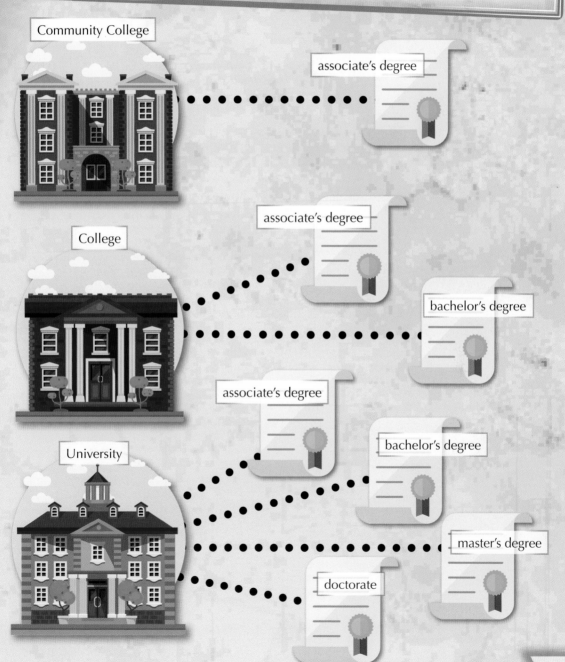

Community College

associate's degree

College

associate's degree

bachelor's degree

University

associate's degree

bachelor's degree

master's degree

doctorate

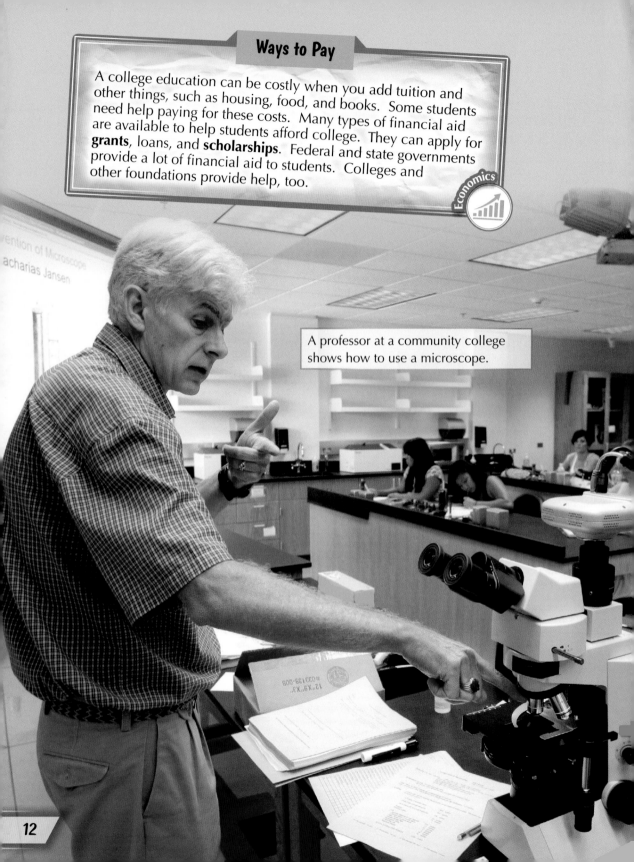

Ways to Pay

A college education can be costly when you add tuition and other things, such as housing, food, and books. Some students need help paying for these costs. Many types of financial aid are available to help students afford college. They can apply for **grants**, loans, and **scholarships**. Federal and state governments provide a lot of financial aid to students. Colleges and other foundations provide help, too.

Economics

A professor at a community college shows how to use a microscope.

Community College

There are 113 community colleges in the state. That is more than any other state in the country. Each year, more than two million students go to community colleges in the state. These schools are a great choice. Some students are not sure what they want to study. They go to community colleges to figure out what they want to learn. Others know what they want to do. They usually attend community colleges for two years. They earn licenses or associate's degrees in nursing or other fields.

Some students study at community colleges for two or three years. Then, they **transfer** to state or private colleges. Their time at community colleges helps them save money. One out of three UC graduates started at a community college in the state. Half of CSU graduates started there, too. For many students, this is a great way to get a college education.

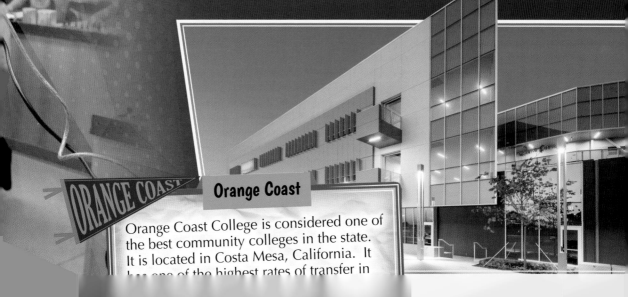

Orange Coast

Orange Coast College is considered one of the best community colleges in the state. It is located in Costa Mesa, California. It has one of the highest rates of transfer in

State Schools

There are two types of state schools: CSU and UC. The CSU system began as individual schools that were not linked in any way. These schools were used to train teachers. Over the years, the schools branched out to teach more subjects. Then, in 1960, the schools combined to form one system.

Today, 23 campuses are part of the CSU system. They stretch from San Diego in the south to Humboldt in the north. Hundreds of thousands of students take classes at CSU campuses each year. The CSU system is the largest public four-year university system in the country.

In 2013, the CSU system began a new **initiative**. It now offers online courses for all students. That was something that had never been done before on such a large scale. Now, there is a wide range of courses to choose from. So, students can find the best fits for them.

From CSU to UC

Author Gary Soto was studying at CSU Fresno when he came across a book of poems in the library. The book awakened Soto's love of writing. He published his first book of poetry in 1977. He went on to write more poetry and stories. Many of them are based on his life growing up as a Mexican American.

FRESNO STATE

Family Firsts

One out of every three CSU students is a first-generation college student. That means they are the first people in their families to go to college. This is a huge achievement. But it can be hard for those students to pave the way. Luckily, staff at the CSU schools make sure all students have the support they need to complete their higher educations.

In 1855, the College of California opened in Oakland. It was a small private school. As the school grew, the building quickly became too small. So, the college **merged** with a state school. The new school became UC Berkeley. It was the first of the UC campuses. The UC system has grown a lot since those early days. Today, it is made up of 10 schools. More than 238,000 students take classes at UC schools each year.

The UC system has three national labs. Students there work with the government to study new forms of **energy**. The UC system also has six medical centers. Students who want to be doctors can learn there. If students do not want to be scientists or doctors, there is still a place for them. The UC system offers more than 150 **disciplines**. UC students can study all kinds of subjects, such as chemistry, art, music, history, and English.

Nobel Prize

Nobel Nods at UC

The Nobel Prize is given to people and groups who have done important work in the world. The award began in 1901. Since then, there have been over 800 winners. Almost 60 winners have been connected to UC schools.

Top Ranks

In 2016, *Money* magazine made a list of the top 100 schools in the country. The magazine looked at schools that offered the best values. The list named five UC campuses to the top 20. UC Berkeley ranked the highest, at number five. San Diego, Irvine, Davis, and Los Angeles also earned top spots.

Humboldt

Chico

Sonoma   Davis   Sacramento

Maritime

Berkeley

East Bay

San Francisco   Stanislaus

San Jose   Merced

Santa Cruz

Monterey Bay   Fresno

Key
- University of California (UC)
- California State University (CSU)
- Both

San Luis Obispo   Bakersfield

Santa Barbara   Pomona

Channel Islands   Northridge   San Bernardino

Los Angeles   Riverside

Dominguez Hills   Fullerton

Long Beach   Irvine

San Marcos

San Diego

Private Colleges and Universities

There are 185 private colleges in California. Going to school at one costs more than going to a state college. Some students think the cost is worth it. Some private schools focus on one subject. They may teach religion, mathematics, or art. Or, they might focus on a small group of subjects, such as research or **liberal arts**. Other private schools just offer classes online.

Lights, Camera, Action!

USC is famous for its film program. It began in 1929 as the first one in the country. Many actors, directors, and producers from USC have won awards for their work.

USC campus in 1910

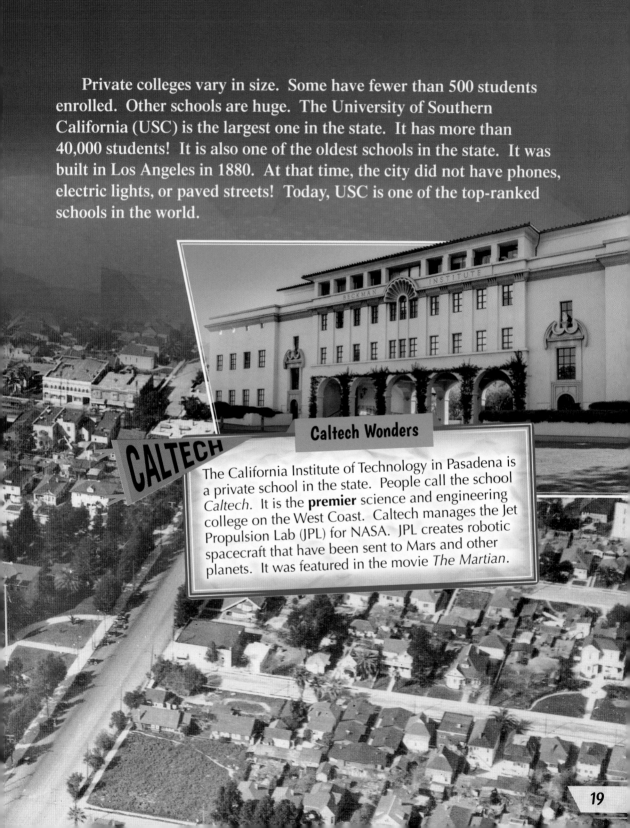

Private colleges vary in size. Some have fewer than 500 students enrolled. Other schools are huge. The University of Southern California (USC) is the largest one in the state. It has more than 40,000 students! It is also one of the oldest schools in the state. It was built in Los Angeles in 1880. At that time, the city did not have phones, electric lights, or paved streets! Today, USC is one of the top-ranked schools in the world.

CALTECH

Caltech Wonders

The California Institute of Technology in Pasadena is a private school in the state. People call the school *Caltech*. It is the **premier** science and engineering college on the West Coast. Caltech manages the Jet Propulsion Lab (JPL) for NASA. JPL creates robotic spacecraft that have been sent to Mars and other planets. It was featured in the movie *The Martian*.

College Competitors

Whether they go to state or private colleges, most students have a lot of school pride. This pride leads to some schools becoming **rivals**. Students take these rivalries very seriously. They may choose to go to a school just because of a rivalry. They spend their time at school trying to be better than their rivals.

Battle of the North

One of the oldest rivalries is between two of the state's oldest colleges. Stanford University and UC Berkeley have competed for many years. The students **strive** to make their schools the best. Even the sports teams are rivals. When their football teams play, it is called the *Big Game*. The first match was held in 1892. It is one of the oldest sports competitions in the state.

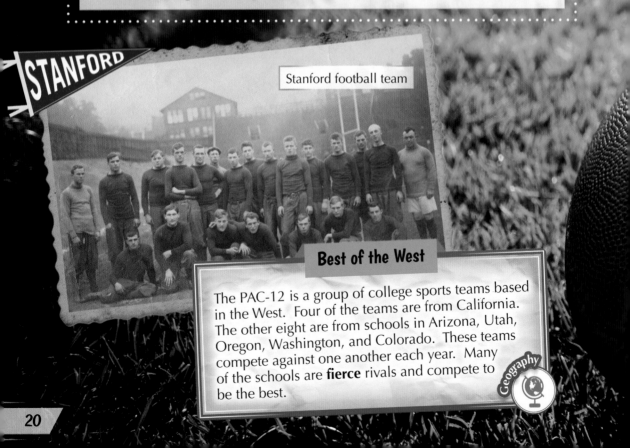

STANFORD

Stanford football team

Best of the West

The PAC-12 is a group of college sports teams based in the West. Four of the teams are from California. The other eight are from schools in Arizona, Utah, Oregon, Washington, and Colorado. These teams compete against one another each year. Many of the schools are **fierce** rivals and compete to be the best.

Geography

Give Them the Axe

In 1899, Berkeley students stole an axe at a college baseball game. Stanford students were using the axe to lead their fans in cheers. The Berkeley students stole it after the game. A wild chase through the streets of San Francisco took place before they got away. The axe was kept at the UC campus for 31 years before it was stolen back. Today, the axe is used as a trophy for the Big Game.

UC BERKELEY

Crosstown Rivals

Los Angeles is home to one of the fiercest rivalries in the country. Students at UC Los Angeles (UCLA) and USC have competed since the 1920s. The two campuses are less than 20 miles (32 kilometers) apart from one another. But they are far from friendly neighbors.

Sports play a big part in this rivalry. Since 2001, the two schools have competed for the Crosstown Cup. Each time the schools face each other in a sporting event, the students keep track of the winner. At the end of the year, the school with the most wins from the year gets the Cup.

The rivalry does not end with sports. Both USC and UCLA have strong medical programs. And they are both research universities. Students compete to win the most awards in those fields, too.

UCLA Sports Star

Jackie Robinson was the first African American to play in Major League Baseball. Before he crossed that hurdle, he was leaping over other ones. As a student at UCLA, he played four sports. He was on the baseball, football, and basketball teams. And he was a track star.

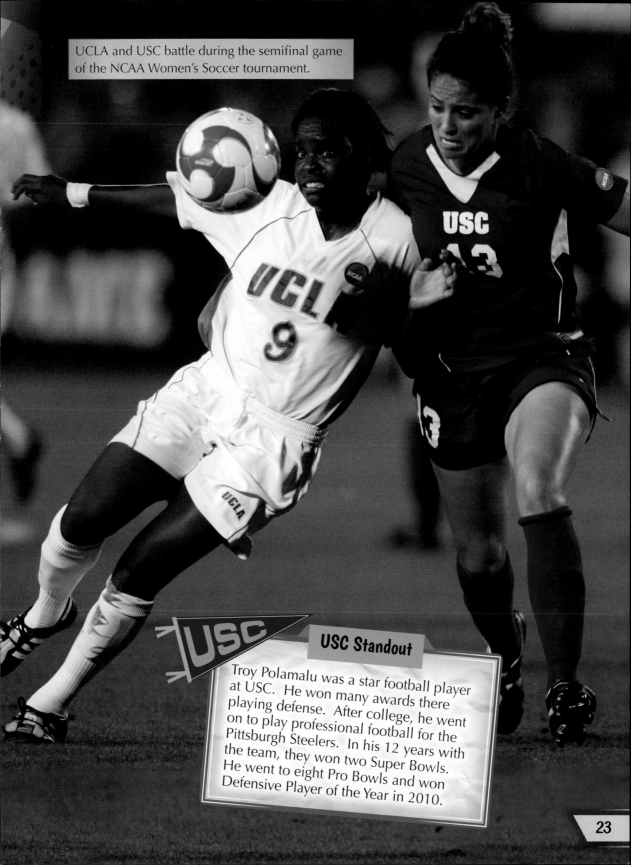

UCLA and USC battle during the semifinal game of the NCAA Women's Soccer tournament.

USC Standout

Troy Polamalu was a star football player at USC. He won many awards there playing defense. After college, he went on to play professional football for the Pittsburgh Steelers. In his 12 years with the team, they won two Super Bowls. He went to eight Pro Bowls and won Defensive Player of the Year in 2010.

Warriors and Tails

SDSU's school **mascot** is the Aztec Warrior. The Aztecs were a civilization based in Mexico and were considered to be one of the most advanced peoples of their time. UCSD's mascot is King Triton. Triton is a Greek god of the sea who has a tail instead of legs and carries a trident.

Hepner Hall is one of the oldest buildings on the SDSU campus.

Young vs. Old

Farther south, another rivalry has caused residents of San Diego to choose sides. San Diego State University (SDSU) is part of the CSU system. UC San Diego (UCSD) is just north of SDSU. UCSD is a much younger school than its rival. SDSU was built in 1897. It is the oldest and largest university in San Diego. UCSD did not open its doors until 1960. It is known as the "younger brother" school in San Diego.

Today, SDSU and UCSD have around 35,000 students each. The two schools do not play each other often in sports. But when they do meet, students loudly support their schools. Chants of "younger brother" are shouted from the SDSU side. It is met with a roaring, "I believe that we will win," from the UCSD fans. Both teams want to be the best that San Diego has to offer.

Director Ochoa

In 1993, Ellen Ochoa became the first Hispanic woman to go to space. After three more trips, she was named the director of the Johnson Space Center. Ochoa says she owes all of her success to her "good educational background." What is that background? Part of it was spent at SDSU.

A College for Every Student

There is a college for every student in California. Each school is great in its own way. The settlers were right all those years ago. Education is important. It has helped make California a great state.

Whichever school a student picks, he or she will receive a great education. Picking the right school comes down to what you hope to come away with. If a student wants to learn a little bit about a lot of things, a community college might be the best start. Other students might want to learn a lot about just one thing. That is where state and private colleges can help.

No matter what you want to do in life, education plays a key role. Education helps people learn new skills to reach their dreams. So, study hard!

The Claremont Colleges

About 35 miles (56 kilometers) east of Los Angeles is the city of Claremont. It is home to a **consortium** of five small private schools. The schools share many resources like dining halls and libraries. Students can take classes at any of the campuses. Pomona College is the oldest school. Scripps College is a women's college. Pitzer College, Harvey Mudd College, and Claremont McKenna College are the other schools in the consortium.

Graduation is an exciting time. Here, students at UCLA celebrate their accomplishments.

Blog It!

How can you decide which college or university is best for you? First, research some options. Think about what is important to you. Do you want to study one subject? Or do you want to learn many different things? Do you want art, music, or literature to be the focus of your school? Are you more interested in science and math? Where do you want to live?

After you pick a school, write a blog post defending your position. Try to convince your friends to go to your school. Then, trade papers with classmates and read about their choices. Do you still think you made the best choice? If not, write a new blog post about why your new choice will be a better fit.

POMONA COLLEGE

LET ONLY THE
EACER THOVGHTFVL
AND REVERENT
ENTER HERE

Glossary

consortium—a group that has agreed to share resources and has the same purpose

crucial—very important

degrees—documents given to people who have graduated from a school of higher education

delegate—a person chosen to speak for a state in making new laws and decisions about that state

disciplines—areas of study

energy—power that comes from a source, such as heat, electricity, wind, or the sun

evolved—developed from something else

fierce—having intense and aggressive behaviors

grants—amounts of money given to people to be used to fund projects

initiative—a program or plan designed to solve some problem

liberal arts—a focus on a small group of subjects, such as literature, history, foreign language, sciences, and math

mascot—a person, object, or animal that is used as a symbol to represent a group

merged—caused two things to combine into one thing

premier—most important

rivals—people or teams that compete with others

scholarships—amounts of money given to people to help pay for their educations

segregation—the practice of separating groups based on their race or religion

strive—to try very hard to do something

transfer—to move to a different place or situation

tuition—money that is paid to a school to study there

Index

Your Turn!

A Special Speech

Many graduates give speeches that describe how their experiences at school have shaped the way they see the world. If you were to give a graduation speech to your classmates, what would you say? Write a speech describing your favorite moments with teachers and classmates in school. How have they helped you in and out of the classroom?